Rising Strong

by Brene Brown

Summary & Analysis

By Instaread

Please Note

This is a key takeaways and analysis.

Table of Contents

OVERVIEW

Rising Strong: the Reckoning, the Rumble, the Revolution by Brene Brown is a book about the importance of people getting back up after they have fallen. But it is also a book about the way they should bounce back. The author has a specific approach to bouncing back that, if followed, will make those who rise again stronger from what they were before they stumbled.

She calls the three steps to her approach the Reckoning, the Rumble, or Owning Our Story, and the Revolution. The Reckoning is recognizing that people are feeling emotion from a fall and want to know where the emotion is rooted, where it is coming from. The Rumble is the step when people challenge the initial stories they have concocted about the fall and try to achieve the real truth of what happened. The Revolution is the step where people transform themselves and grow from what they learned from the fall.

Brown's approach is for those who take a fall to examine the emotions that the stumble unleashed in them so they can try to understand what really caused the fall because those emotions often betray the real story. Those who suffer a fall make up their own account of what happened that does not reflect reality. For example, they may say that someone else caused their fall, and actually believe it. Or they may blame themselves when they were not at fault. Or they may even come up with a conspiracy theory about what was behind their fall.

Only after reflecting on the situation with an eye toward arriving at the truth of what happened can they come up with the correct story. Once they have that story, they need to use what they learned while coming to that realization to connect better with others and live a more wholehearted life, which is to be a better spouse, parent, and colleague. In other words, they need to emerge from the fall a better, more rounded, and more empathetic.

IMPORTANT PEOPLE

Brene Brown: The author of *Rising Strong,* is a University of Houston social work professor and psychology researcher. She tells a lot of stories about situations in her own life to illustrate key points in the book.

Steve Alley: Brene Brown's husband, Alley is a pediatrician who figures prominently in many stories in the book. He often brings wisdom that helps Brown understand emotions she is feeling about situations she is involved in, or helps her arrive at a framework for understanding a situation.

Diana: Diana is Brown's therapist. Brown often mentions her therapy sessions in the book when discussing personal epiphanies concerning her emotions.

Jean Kantambu Latting: Jean Kantambu Latting was one of Brown's professors and dissertation advisors. Latting is one of the author's most influential mentors.

Claudia: Claudia had a rough experience with her alcoholic sister. Brown uses this situation to help teach her method of overcoming a fall.

Pamela: Pamela sent a hateful email to Brown, causing her to learn about shame during a therapy session.

Ellen and Charlie: Brown's children, Ellen and Charlie, also figure in several of Brown's stories in *Rising Strong.*

KEY TAKEAWAYS

1. Everyone falls. People need to learn to rise again in a way that transforms them into more wholehearted people.

2. The Reckoning which is the first step in rising from a fall is recognizing the emotion connected with the fall, then trying to understand what the emotion means.

3. The Rumbling which is the second step in rising from a fall is examining the first story the person told themselves about why they fell and, if they made up the story, seeking the truth.

4. The Revolution which is the third step in rising from a fall is arriving at the real story about why the person fell, and using the story to help achieve a better connection with the world and a more wholehearted life.

5. A person should be generous toward others they initially might want to blame for their fall, believing they are doing the best they can with their life.

6. It is important to understand that a range of emotions may get in the way of arriving at the truth about why a person fell. Acknowledging and managing these emotions makes it easier for people to get to the truth.

7. It is also important, when seeking the truth of why a person fell, to understand that people bring their own prism to the assessment process, including the lenses of shame, perfectionism, values, and regret.

8. It is important that a person be ready to ask for help when they fall rather than trying to bounce back on their own.

ANALYSIS OF KEY TAKEAWAYS

Key Takeaway 1

Everyone falls. People need to learn to rise again in a way that transforms them into more wholehearted people.

Analysis

Many people show courage by taking on a difficult task or trying something they have never done before. Sometimes they succeed beyond their wildest dreams, with everything going as planned. Other times, they fall. How they emerge from the fall says a lot about who they will be in the future and whether they will continue their personal development. If they can understand what really caused the fall, even if obtaining the understanding is difficult, they will grow as a person.

Greg Mathis' transformation from heroin dealer and gang member to judge and television show personality is an inspirational story of how to rise from a fall. Mathis drew up in a tough neighborhood of Detroit, and fell in with the wrong crowd. Before he was 17, he spent time in juvenile detention. Finally, one judge had enough. He ordered Mathis to get a high school diploma or go to prison. The ultimatum came just before Mathis learned his mother was dying of cancer. He promised her that he would get his life back on track. Mathis could have blamed others for the troubled person he had become, such as the police, the system, or the lack of a father. But he did not. He ended up getting a law degree and being elected the youngest judge in Michigan history. He then served many years as a Michigan Superior Court judge, a post from which he retired. Television programs featuring real judges had become popular in the United States with the show, *Judge Judy*. In 1999, a television production company asked Mathis to be the title judge on a show involving a small claims court format. Thanks to the show, *Judge Mathis*, his adept handling of cases, and the fact that he overcame a difficult childhood, made him a role model in the African-American community [1].

Key Takeaway 2

The Reckoning which is the first step in rising from a fall is recognizing the emotion connected with the fall, then trying to understand what the emotion means.

Analysis

When people fall, they cannot help but become emotional. A fall always hurts, so two emotions those who have fallen almost always feel are disappointment and pain. But they might also feel shame, resentment, anger, fear, and many other emotions. It is important that they sort out these emotions by identifying what they are. Once they understand what emotions are at play, they need to identify what is behind them. In the case of anger, for instance, they need to figure out if they are angry with themselves or with others.

Take the theoretical example of Jane, a city editor at a newspaper. Her boss Jack, the managing editor, demands to know why the newspaper missed a story about a double homicide the day before. Jane is angry after Jack dresses her down. However, she must decide who she is really angry with. Her first instinct is to be angry with Jack as he is too demanding and puts too much pressure on her. She only became city editor three months ago. It is a tough job with a steep learning curve, and she is not where she wants to be yet. Even though Jack is a demanding boss, she decides it is unfair to be angry with him as he is just doing his job. Hashing out the situation some more, she decides she is angry with the police-beat reporter as it was his job to be on top of breaking crime stories. Jane is reflecting, trying to build a bridge between the emotion she is feeling about her fall and what actually happened in the fall, rather than a story she made up about what happened. She has yet to finish piecing together a true account of her fall, but she is getting closer.

14

Key Takeaway 3

The Rumbling which is the second step in rising from a fall is examining the first story the person told themselves about why they fell and, if they made up the story, seeking the truth.

Analysis

Everyone makes up stories about why they fall. Those accounts are often shaped by fears, prejudices, and the way people would like to see the world rather than the way it actually is. In many cases, a person's initial account of a fall, even if it is the wrong account, is the one they stick with. And that account often involves blaming others for what happened. A person who seeks the real meaning from a fall will examine their initial story and, if it is wrong, discard it, and try to come up with the truth.

Jane, the city editor, decided to continue reflecting to try to identify the real reason why her newspaper missed the double homicide story. The first story she made up about her fall was that it was Jack's fault because he was too demanding as a boss. Nobody can ever meet his expectations. But, deep inside, she knew his demanding ways were not the reason for her stumble. She then shifted the focus to Jimmy, the rookie police beat reporter. Upon further reflection, she realized she was angry with herself, not Jimmy. He had been covering the police beat only six days and had yet to meet all of the officers, including the ones who could have tipped him to the double homicide story. In fact, Jimmy asked Jane if the previous police reporter could give him more orientation before he took over the beat on his own. If the fall that Jane took was not Jack or Jimmy's fault, she must continue to figure out whose fault it was. She wondered if it was her, a set of circumstances she could not have predicted, both her and unforeseen circumstances, or something else.

Key Takeaway 4

The Revolution which is the third step in rising from a fall is arriving at the real story about why the person fell, and using the story to help achieve a better connection with the world and a more wholehearted life.

Analysis

It usually takes time to come up with the real story about why a person fell. The first story a person concocts is likely to be off the mark. Often those who stumble create the first version of their story hastily to help themselves cope with the emotional fallout from what happened. The second, revised story that they concoct may be closer to the truth, but still not squarely on target. Revising the story to convey the truth of the fall is the point at which a person begins growing from their stumble.

In the case of the missed double homicide story, Jane came to realize that the person responsible for her fall was her. She breathed a sigh of relief, thankful she had not dressed Jimmy down. She realized she needed to be a better manager of both the newsroom process and the people in it In terms of process, she decided to ask the staff what kind of orientation and training they needed to do their jobs, and to create a system for giving them this information. She also recognized that she had been trying to be a perfectionist, one manifestation of which was her setting impossible standards for her staff. While still setting the bar high, she became less uptight about the mistakes the newsroom made. She also began admitting when she made a mistake. The staff loved the change they saw in her. They became more willing to take risks to get a story. They also began admitting their mistakes and asking Jane for feedback on how they could do better next time. Noticing her new rapport with the staff, Jane also decided to take a new approach with her boss. She leveled with him. She told Jack that, while she was pretty good at what she did, it was impossible for her to prevent the news operation from making an occasional mistake. Jack appreciated her candor. They began working better together, and developed a mutually supportive relationship.

Key Takeaway 5

A person should be generous toward others they initially might want to blame for their fall, believing they are doing the best they can with their life.

Analysis

The question of whether everyone is doing the best they can with their lives is hotly debated. *Rising Strong* author Brene Brown is aware that more and more psychologists and human-relationship experts are maintaining that people are doing their best. She was a skeptic, but once she examined the issue closely, became a believer. The lesson from this, in terms of rising from our a fall, is that because people are doing the best they can, people should not rush to blame them for our stumble.

Brown let an acquaintance really get under her skin. The woman pointed out in an email that Brown had mispronounced a well-known person's name during a speech. Brown was incensed about what she thought was the woman's mean-spirited, deliberate attempt to hurt her. It took Brown weeks of thought and talking with others to decide that the woman really was doing the best she could rather than going out of her way to hurt Brown deliberately. Adam Brady, who is associated with the Chopra Center that teaches a self-awareness approach to wellbeing, offers tips on how people can prevent themselves from being hurt by the kind of difficult person Brown dealt with. One tip is not to take an unpleasant encounter with such a person personally. It is likely that the encounter was not a thought-out, deliberately planned attack. If people take such encounters personally, they feel anger, stress, and other negative emotions, and they become defensive, which generates additional negative emotions. Another Brady tip is to try to see an unpleasant encounter with someone else as a learning experience. This is actually what Brown ended up doing. Brady said that a person who has gone through an unpleasant encounter should ask themselves what the encounter was meant to teach them. It may be something about their own character, including something they do not want to see. By seeing the encounter as a learning experience, the person who was on the receiving end of the unpleasantness can let go of their negative emotions and also grow as a person [2].

Key Takeaway 6

It is important to understand that a range of emotions may get in the way of arriving at the truth about why a person fell. Acknowledging and managing these emotions makes it easier for people to get to the truth.

Analysis

Almost every human emotion can come into play when people try to rise from a fall. They include disappointment, anger, resentment, self-loathing, heartbreak, grief, connection, forgiveness, compassion, and empathy. These swirling emotions can cast a fog over clear thinking, making it difficult for people to see the truth about why they fell. Understanding that these emotions exist, and identifying which ones are in play, makes it easier for people to cut through the fog so they can arrive at the truth of the fall.

Professor Mike A. Shepherd talks about how emotions after a fall can make it harder for business people to learn from their mistakes. In his book *From Lemons from Lemonade: Squeeze Every Last Drop Out of Your Mistakes*, Shepherd discusses the emotions that hampered his father's bounce back from the loss of his business. They included numbness and disbelief that he had lost the company, and anger about the poor economic climate and the role that competitors and creditors may have played in the company's demise. Other emotions included guilt and self-loathing. Shepherd's father wanted to pass the business on to another son, but he could not, so he also felt he was a failure as both a businessman and a father. These emotions made it harder for Shepherd's father to get his life back on track and emerge stronger from his fall. The good news was that he did bounce back, and his difficult experience led to personal growth. Many people think that learning from failure is instantaneous,. It is not. It takes time. But it can be managed, starting with sorting out the emotions that are in play in a fall [3].

Key Takeaway 7

It is also important, when seeking the truth of why a person fell, to understand that people bring their own prism to the assessment process, including the lenses of shame, perfectionism, values, and regret.

Analysis

Everyone views situations through the filter of personal experience. What happened to someone in the past shapes the way they view what is happening to them today and will happen to them in the future. It is important that people try to recognize these filters, and put them aside, when they are trying to make sense of a fall. For example, shame can be a powerful filter. It can color any objective examination of what happened when a person fell, preventing them from getting at the truth.

One of the filters that can come into play in a fall is values. Everyone has a set of values, but they differ from person to person based on a person's upbringing, culture, and several other factors. Many scholars have studied the differences that cultural values bring to assessments and decision making. African-Americans have long complained that the predominantly white news media has given members of African-American community overwhelmingly negative coverage compared with other ethnic groups, whose coverage appears more balanced. Beginning in the 1960s, the news media began taking this complaint to heart by hiring African-American journalists. The reasoning was that these journalists would help bring a more balanced picture of African-Americans to news reports, changing the negative view that many whites had of blacks.

African-Americans and other ethnic groups are likely to assess their falls differently from whites because their upbringings and cultural values are different. It is important, when people are assessing how they fell to consider whether their cultural values are preventing them from reaching an objective assessment of what happened. This would be particularly true in cases where a fall involved an interaction between the person who fell and a member of another ethnic group. Although it is hard to set aside a person's cultural values when assessing a fall, being able to do so can help get the person who fell closer to the truth of what happened [4].

Key Takeaway 8

It is important that a person be ready to ask for help when they fall rather than trying to bounce back on their own.

Analysis

Everyone falls. People can manage a lot of small stumbles by themselves. But some falls are so devastating or vexing that it would be better for people to ask for help in addressing them. This does not constitute weakness. On the contrary, it shows strength because the person is willing to do what it takes after a fall to achieve the most wholehearted outcome for themselves. The helper a person chooses does not have to be a psychiatrist, school counselor, or pastor. It can be a spouse, relative, or friend. The key is that it must be someone the person can trust, someone who will keep the information they tell them confidential, and who will not use it as a weapon against them later.

The notion of group therapy hinges on the idea that in many instances it is better for people to try to emerge from a fall with help rather than go it alone. One of the oldest group therapy organizations is Alcoholics Anonymous, founded in 1933 in Akron, Ohio. The key goals of the program were for members to stay sober and help other alcoholics quit drinking and stay sober. The organization's founders, Bill Wilson and Dr. Bob Smith, both of whom were alcoholics, recognized from their own lives how difficult it is for problem drinkers to quit and, once they do, stop themselves from reverting back to drinking. They contended that this required a change in the way alcoholics thought about life. Wilson and Smith believed that group support rather than going it alone was a better way for alcoholics to change their thinking and remain sober. The idea was that members of the group could help those who were struggling with encouragement, their own stories, and suggestions. Alcoholics Anonymous keeps record of the success of its program. The main yardstick is how long a person remained sober after starting the program. In 2014, the organization reported that 22 percent of its members had been sober more than 20 years, 14 percent had been sober between 10 and 20 years, 13 percent between five and 10 years, 24 percent one to five years, and 27 percent less than a year. These results, plus the organization's longevity, suggest that it has helped a lot of alcoholics who might have slipped back into drink remain sober [5].

AUTHOR'S STYLE

Brene Brown's style in *Rising Strong* is easy on the reader. Everyone loves stories, and she decided that most of the lessons she wanted to convey in the book lent themselves to storytelling. So that is her main literary device.

To help her make her points, she also mentions research she has conducted, but there are not nearly as many references to research as in her other three books. She also offers ideas from other scholars and researchers. These mentions are scattered through the book, so there is no collective overdose of experts.

Most of the stories Brown tells are about her. She conveys them with emotion because she remembers the feelings they invoked in her and the lessons she learned from each of the situations she writes about. The stories involve her childhood, her relationship with her husband, Steve, and their children, Ellen and Charlie, her relationship with other relatives, some of whom are colorful characters, her interactions with helpful colleagues, her run-ins with hurtful acquaintances, and her interactions with strangers, including homeless people.

After telling one or more stories about a particular topic, Brown pulls them all together to summarize the lessons she is trying to convey with a story or set of stories. The summaries are clear, insightful, and thought-provoking.

PERSPECTIVE

Brene Brown is a University of Houston social work professor who has done widely acclaimed work on vulnerability. Her work has led to her publishing four book that deal with psychology and human relationships, and becoming a much sought after speaker. Two of her books, *The Gifts of Imperfection* and *Daring Greatly*, were New York Times bestsellers. Her insight into the human condition has led to guest appearances on *Oprah* and other television shows. Although all of Brown's works are rooted in vulnerability, she has branched into other topics, including the best approach to rising from a fall that is the subject of *Rising Strong.*

~~~~~~ END OF INSTAREAD~~~~~~

REFERENCES

1. "Judge Mathis," Wikipedia, accessed August 28, 2015, https://en.wikipedia.org/wiki/Judge_Mathis.

2. Brady, Adams, "7 Steps for Dealing With Difficult People," www.chopra.com, accessed August 28, 2015, http://www.chopra.com/ccl/7-steps-for-dealing-with-difficult-people.

3. Shepherd, Dean A., www.ftpress.com, accessed August 28, 2015, http://www.ftpress.com/articles/article.aspx?p=1329142.

4. "Difference in Cultures," www.analytictech.com, accessed August 28, 2015, http://www.analytictech.com/mb021/cultural.htm.

5. "Alcoholics Anonymous," en.wikipedia.org, accessed August 28, 2015, https://en.wikipedia.org/wiki/Alcoholics_Anonymous.

Lightning Source UK Ltd.
Milton Keynes UK
UKHW02f1028270218
318552UK00007B/1075/P